THE MAKINGS OF YOU

ACKNOWLEDGEMENTS

Versions of the following poems have been published or broadcast previously:
"Half-a-Lime" in *Diverse-city,* the Austin International Poetry Festival Journal, 2005; "Destination DC (w/Mom)", "Ballast I" and "By yourself, boy…" in the *Oregon Literary Review*; "Stripping the Yam" on BBC Radio – World Service; "Ballast III" in *The Liberal*; "The Fall" in *Poetry Review*; "Ballast IV" in *Warpland Journal* (Chicago State University); "E be So", "Daybreak at Swanlake", "Lapse" and "Rich Tea" in *Wasafiri*.

NII AYIKWEI PARKES

THE MAKINGS OF YOU

Poetry series editor: Kwame Dawes

PEEPAL TREE

First published in Great Britain in 2010
Peepal Tree Press Ltd
17 King's Avenue
Leeds LS6 1QS
UK

ISBN 13: 9781845231590

Supported by
ARTS COUNCIL
ENGLAND

CONTENTS

1

E Be So	9
Transit	10
Permissible Neurosis	11
Gardening	12
One Against Three	13
Rich Tea	15
Shields and Shadow	16
The One About the Man	17
Freeze Frame	18
Lapse	19
Barter	20
Half-a-Lime	21
Unilateral	23
The Makings of You	25
À La Carte	27
Destination DC from Ghana (w/Mom)	28
Crossing Borders	30
Zion Train	32
Background	33

2

Ayitey, 1973	37
Pebbles, 1980	39
The Fall, 1983	41
The Rainy Season, 1984	43
The Fall of Man	44
Wings, 1987	46
The Cut	48
Jerry, 1999	51
By Yourself, Boy (1988-2007)	52
Stripping the Yam	54

3

Ballast I: A Generous Courier   61
Ballast II: The Birth of Liquid Desire   62
Ballast III: Turtle in the Sky   63
Ballast IV: Flung Out Like a Fag-end   64
Ballast V: The Persistence of Memory   65
Ballast VI: Fancy   66
Ballast VII: Steps   67
Ballast VIII: Pepper   68
Ballast IX: Pool   69
Ballast X: Final Cries   70

4

draughts, ephemera, factions   73
Circus   75
What I Know   77
Men Like Me   78
Faith   79
Daydreaming   80
Dinner for One   81
Inclination   82
Interjection   83
The Snake's Revenge   84
A Familiar Voice at the V&A Museum   86
Rebellion   88
The Princess and the Pea   89
Fading to Wild   90

1

"I been in the blues all my life. I'm still delivering 'cause I got a long memory."

— Muddy Waters

E BE SO

(Red, Accra, 1980)

"We have come to the cross-roads
And I must either leave or come with you." — Kwesi Brew ("The Mesh")

E be so we dey do am for here. He digs
a knife-wide hole in the ground
and looks up at me, his eyes two worlds
colliding. I stand two feet back trying to conjure
the streets of South London, holding onto
my six-year-old nonchalance in the face of death.

I hear say pipol for abroad dey shock them
plus lactric, but for here e be so we dey
do am. The chickens stop squawking
the moment Red squats, watching from a distance
as he prepares to cull their number. *Make you*
close your eyes. I do, but he pulls me forward
to see the white bird shut its eyes obediently
as he steps on its feet and wings.

You see, de hole be where de blood go go
e be for the pipol for de other side. You
for no kill chicken by heart, you hear? He wipes
the blade on yellowed feathers, slits the neck
quickly, then holds the twitching body
over the hole until it stills, empty of fight.

After only nine months living in Accra, this is
initiation. Red is my living guide, my mystic.
I stare at the black hole beneath my feet,
still warm with blood, then at the eight
chickens lined up like fresh Gladiators,
beginning to scratch the soil for prey, then
I hear him say: *Next time e be you go kill am,*
e be so we dey do am for here.

TRANSIT

A girl walks by, leaves the air thick
with the scent of cocoa butter; an *abuela*
places a half-drunk can of soda in her bag –

complete with straw – while smiling at her
granddaughter; a junkie scratches and talks
fast, believes he's still slick enough to lure

a woman with a quick flick of the comb
he keeps in the stretch of his socks.
I catch a whiff of nail varnish, spy

the balancing lean of a woman painting
her nails in the subway. Vanity is casual
and love, it seems, the price of a wide smile

cast across the length or breadth of a carriage:
father to daughter, woman to man, stranger to
stranger, as the rumble moves from darkness

into the unknown, another station, void.

PERMISSIBLE NEUROSIS

This is where I tell you my Grandma died
in our arms – my mother, brother and I –
while my father fumbled with car keys, hope
pulsing in his eyes, that he could still buy
her a few more years if he could just fly
past traffic to the hospital.
                                    No soap
could dramatise his son's belief that Mum
would not leave – that if he called she would come.

Then, of course,
                        there's the women I was sure
were using me for kicks,
                                    the lecturer
we proved marked me down because I was black,

the drought, the bailiffs... *The craic?*

Well, I want you to tell me I'm not ill;
that my neurosis is permissible.

GARDENING

A habit inherited: this fumbling
with God's mass, turning it and readying it
for sowing. An inbred twilight twinge
that propels me to my patch where I tend
green-skinned tomatoes and watch my carrots
edge their orange heads above the rim of the soil.

At five a.m. there is nothing to see;
only sounds stir: the moans of new couples,
mothers coaxing their broods alive, brooms kissing
the soiled skin of courtyards and, in our time,
your earthbound voice making seeds, bulbs
and crop rotation sound familiar to me.

Your sister once said I sounded like you.
And I wonder, now you've gone to ground,
how you must have felt those mornings in the mist,
watching the seed you planted in a bed of moans
reach for you with muddy fingers, smiling
and speaking to you in a voice you lost many years ago.

ONE AGAINST THREE

I

Fading dark, chorus of trees,
the metal standpipe gaining shape
with sunrise as the cocks begin
to feather the air with sound.

Bucket in hand, I breathe in slow
memory of early morning stretching
– of limbs in exercise, lips
in smiles, breath in effort.

II

In the headstand, Daddy's speech
is inverted without losing meaning:
It's in the breathing, he says,
it's the key to everything.

He winks as we bend into shapes
illustrated with clear thin lines
in a wide green book of yoga, its pages
as jaundiced as the coming light.

III

I hold those years of twilight discipline
folded against the sweat of my palms
as three boys corner me. Reticence,
he said, is the best kind of defence;

steel yourself and wait. I exhale,
feel my blood pump – ferric and vital
as the expression of a standpipe,
then wait for the first boy to strike.

RICH TEA

It is an initiation of sorts, I guess,
the sun already raging in the east, with us –
boys and girls – massed in the pre-assembly
hour. The heat is new to me, the glow

edging my Bata sandals, by a distance,
superior to the light I had grown accustomed to
in Grange Park. Also unknown is this boy, who,
with the boldness of an old comrade, spies

a whole biscuit in my right hand and walks up
to me, arms outstretched. He is tall – Christian,
I later find he is called – and one friend more than
I expected on my first day at Ann's Preparatory

School. A borderline cockney myself, I am
staggered by the sharp, muscled edges of his
diction when he speaks: *Give me the biscuit some*
and, a heartbeat later, *please*; his English, like

my Rich Tea, is broken for easier sharing.

SHIELDS AND SHADOWS

Ask my mother
and she will hesitantly tell
how in my second week at school
my classmates came armed.

What in week one was curiosity
had reached the ears of mothers
and fathers, struck dissonant chords
and left their lips unspeakable.

As children will, the unspeakable
was tapped, vulcanised in whispers
then hurled at me with rubber-stamped venom
in the plimsolled patter of the playground.

My response was a harsh vernacular
of fists, learnt while watching Ali
ensconced in my father's lap, listening
to fevered voices saying "Jab, jab, jab."

The ensuing chaos left my mother
apologising to red-faced parents
while my father smiled a secret slant,
resolving to take us back home to Ghana.

Under Daddy's arm my 4-year-old psyche
was altered forever; I was the warrior
who endured a flurry of spears with nothing
but the dark shield of my African face.

My survival instilled in me a smiling
vulcanised arrogance, a fearlessness of failure
and death. Left me with as much time for them
as my shadow trailing me; faithful, dark, unshakeable.

THE ONE ABOUT THE MAN

I wake up to the sound of your voice one morning to find you gone,
and myself fatherless in a cold room rented from a gentle grey
Jamaican man with an unusual skill for transforming the pale skin of
chickens to a perfect succulent brown with a hint of lime. In the
departing dream we were on our porch in Accra; you just retold the
story of how you, an earnest-faced boy, convinced the old ladies of
Jamestown that the ominous hollows of sewerage pipes being laid by
the Government were part of a plot to take the sea away; sent them
scattering –

limp-fleshed, nimble-footed and loud – to the shore with clanging
empty buckets.

Back in Reading, I reach for the darkness with a yawn and try to recall
the joke you were telling before I snapped awake, sweating in the still
air of my bedsit: Could it be the one about the man, who, struck by
a car, rolled into the zebra crossing to insure himself and triggered
an hour-long argument of: *I was in it* – *No, you weren't*; that made it
amply clear that he wasn't injured? Or the one where one dry, dusty
morning, at the height of the drought of 1983, Ayitey was gypped out
of the money for bread, after waiting one hour in the queue, leaving
us famished and my brother forever distrustful? Maybe Grandma's
favourite; the one about me running from the cross-country truck
driver's monkey that escaped while on heat, hiding behind my
mother and claiming I rushed to her side to protect her? Or the one
where your father beat you with gas tubing until *his* mother chased
him away with her walking stick?

I try to fall asleep again, hoping that the joke will return, thinking all
the while that our jokes weren't really funny, they were just sad stories
we learned to laugh at. And if you taught me anything, it was how
to live with pain

and still carry a smile lightly.

FREEZE FRAME

Man, you had the sleight
of hand, the quick-fingered tricks
that allowed you to finish a card
game with a 9 and claim it was a 6.

Back then I never questioned
you, even when you said you had marks
of experience sprouting on your face –
meaning that we had to trust you

with our money. You were Jack Flash,
man, and the camera never caught you
off guard. I kept pictures though,
and eighteen years of hard looking

has exposed the cracks in your stories.
You were just a boy who got spots
a few years before we did, and used
whatever you were given – for profit.

LAPSE

The Greyhound is late. I've been fast
asleep too long to know why, but the man
beside me – Chinese – tells me what time it is.

He turns to the back-lit maze of his phone, taps
a geometry of buttons, gets lost in an exchange
about auditions and lost opportunities. I look

across the aisle: the big guy with the *Yankees*
cap has struck up a dialogue with the Polish
woman beside him. Her dark eyebrows arch –

an eager pair – in synch under her blond hail; I can
tell she's open; so is he, but he's fearful, hasn't
yet learnt the curved asymmetry of lust. There is

already a lapse between her keenness, his lean
and the speed of his initiative. Somebody should
tell him that if the lapse grows any longer

the door of chance will close – snap in
his face. It's already too late. The bus is
drifting into Harlem, Connecticut a distant memory.

I hear him say, *Excuse me*; he calls his Mom. A pink
rose blooms on the woman's cheek, she looks
outside. I hang my head, exhale, and close

my eyes. The man beside me snaps his phone shut.

BARTER

That first winter alone, the true meaning
of all the classroom rhymes that juggled *snow*
and *go*, old and *cold*, acquired new leanings.
With reluctance I accepted the *faux*
deafness and odd looks my Accra greetings
attracted, but I couldn't quell my deep
yearning for contact, warmth, recognition,
the shape of my renown on someone's lips.

Always the canny youth whose history
entailed life on skeletal meal rations
during the Sahel drought of eighty-three,
I lingered in London *gares* to carry
cases for crocked and senior citizens;
barter for a smile's costless revelry.

HALF-A-LIME

His pen moves as fast as darkness scatters.
Three fleshy creases mark his forehead
as he leans pensively forward
like a question mark filled with life.

> *The cocks have crowed; in the streets*
> *brooms raise dust. I rise early.*

I want to be the first to see him
smile, see his small, white teeth
expose themselves without inhibition
like nudists on a beach of gums.

> *Pigeons gather... the sun summons*
> *its light. I head outside.*

I can see him before I see him;
yesterday's paper to his left,
a pen in his right hand
and sheaves of paper awaiting stains.

> *The dew rises like fleeting*
> *possibilities in the new heat.*

He's waiting. I like the song he hums,
the tenor harmony of a Jimmy Smith solo.
Silent, he passes his clean mug to me.
We'll talk between hot sips of tea.

> *The kettle boils; loaded*
> *bubbles of speech waiting to burst.*

I make two cups: black, no sugar,
with half-a-lime squeezed in each.
His mouth forms a vaginal shape as he sips
the heat, the promise of a new day.

Something warm passes from father to son.
Silence becomes an enduring memory.

And this week, I buy seven perfect limes. One
for every new day. I will slice them in two
each morning, squeeze one half for me, and one
half into an empty cup. For the memories.

UNILATERAL

a)

Down the cemetery path
we heave around his grave
like flies feasting on the rejected.
The assembled buzz with comments,
marking our mother's moist face
– molten with sorrow.

The women watch and wail,
the men tense with concern;
oh, how she cries
how she cries.

By her side,
two on each flank,
we are the departed reborn.
Quadrupled like table legs;
sturdy on the outside,
chipped on the inside.

We hold her up
with our fragile faith
drenched in sunlight;
our misery hung out to dry.

The priest speaks.
Hollow voices rise in song.
Two of us – the older boys – step
forward to help lower him
into the ground. At the priest's signal,
we reach for dust.

b)

Watching her we know her sorrow
is not how much she cries,
it's how the sun illuminates her

because she has no more
light inside her.

THE MAKINGS OF YOU

"Almost impossible to do; describing the makings of you"
— Curtis Mayfield

You will tell no one
of the Christmas day when you sat
alone in your miniscule studio,
raised a forkful of sautéed potato
to your lips, and closed your eyes;

how savouring that mouthful of electric heat
and some farmer's zealous labour, followed
by two hours of reading Neruda and Li-Young
Lee, was your only way of remembering
that life's sack carries pleasure as well as pain.

At that dinner next week you will tell
nothing of how vacuous you felt, nor
will you mention the time when tortured
by your girlfriend's inability to trust you
you drank cheap whiskey and clawed your walls

while singing along to Curtis Mayfield's
the makings of you, as though the song's lush
beauty would save you from depression.
No, you will tell jokes and smile and make
predictably witty and charming comments;

you will tell no one of the day when,
as an ashy-kneed eleven-year-old boy
in boarding school, you surreptitiously
sat on the concrete steps of your classroom
block to pick up a groundnut you had spotted

earlier, cleaned it against your brown shorts
and slipped it in your mouth where you let it sit
for an instant, before you chewed it for six slow
minutes, so you could fool your own stomach
into thinking that life was better than it was.

All these things that make you the man
that you are, you tuck beneath your dark
skin and never share: so nobody really knows
you, although most people say they like you
because of your enigmatic smile.

À LA CARTE

Absorbed in the transparent music
of clinking glasses, I am slashed
back to the mundane by a waiter

handing me a menu ex cathedra
then slinking away as silently
as an espadrille-shoed ghost.

Around me my seven companions
delve feverishly into the textual
mysteries of the folded card, fondling

its ridged paper expectantly
as they debate: chicken, fish or lamb?
I bear a crippled smile as I open

my pleated gift knowing I will be stumped
as I always am by the ambiguity
of culinary lingo; does seared tuna

mean cooked on high heat for three
or five minutes, on one or both sides?
This is why I rarely go to restaurants.

For the same reason I censor the news:
what makes an Iraqi victim unfortunate
and an American one tragic? What makes

Somoza an OK guy, and Castro a vile man?
Is it the same ghost that decides that
Che was a guerrilla, and the lobster is done?

DESTINATION DC FROM GHANA (W/ MOM)

The stench boasts a complex history: fish
sold by the crate at 5 am, endless hours
of work, flights from sadness. Forsyth

and East Broadway — outpost of China
in New York — an overabundance of hope
manifests in the quick speech of a tout

selling coach tickets to the Capitol. My Mom
and I walk with oscillating eyes, seeking
number 88. For us, this is a departure point

— destination DC. I find myself reaching for her
hand; our roles have reversed, I am the one
who says *cross now*, waits for her to catch up.

At the apex of chaos, we buy pink tickets,
clamber up a bus with a Washington DC sign
and take our seats. Two French girls chat

in front of us. One leaves and comes back
bearing three boxes of *Tiger* balm in her palms
like juggling balls. She passes two to her

companion and opens the last to smear
a thin layer in her nostrils. Inhaling, she
offers the jar to my Mom who accepts, then

says *I have the same thing in liquid.* My
Mom has turned from nurse to doctor of aches
and pains; there is no ointment in the world

outside her radar. She defies age with these
concoctions, and splashes of red and brown
in her hair – sparklers in the night. I turn

to our new friends and ask them which part
of Paris they are from. *St Denis*, they say.
I tell them I know it well: *the stadium, right?*

One of my best friends is from there. Patrice?
Oh, my God! We went to school with him. A thin
line of pleasure bloods my mother's face; this

is how my father was, a curious traveller, falcons
for eyes, his brain a compendium of the random,
finding connections in every corner of the earth.

CROSSING BORDERS

I can scarcely remember
my first crossing of water,
borders, dare-lines or fingers.

All I have seen is pictures preserved
by Mom
in envelopes and matching albums:

me, in snow, lost in a bright yellow winter coat,
me, skipping careless in some vast green park,
me, exposed to December sand and sun,

my surroundings Sahelian
like old memories.

Flicking through the prints
                    cross-checking dates
of birth, death and travel,
                    I realise that we never travelled
as a unit, a complete family

of mother, three brothers
sister and father – too
late now with one gone.

But imagine the trauma,
the yelling, screaming and laughter
that would have accompanied us

simply because in spite of our common
heritage of cold showers and warm,
cracked grins, heavy breakfasts complemented

by the heft of yesterdays
told in light jovial tones

to the strains of highlife leaking
                    from the neighbour's house;
notwithstanding our united views
                    on love, and our gritty ambition;
despite the lessons we learned

together falling from mango trees,
our multilingual arguments
without pause for sentiment;

regardless of our matching teeth,
easy, yet determined, strides
and the twin glints of our shoes;

by mere accidents of birth,
the post-coital motions of our parents,
some of us would be allowed to cross

certain borders unhindered
others would be stopped

treated like intruders,
                    beggars with no vision,
parasites come to feed
                    off the ailing root
of a dead empire.

ZION TRAIN

Me ketch it so: five-year-old rough-head pickney chanting
No Woman No Cry fe me mother inna de morning;
not cos she crying but cos Bob rolling to roll

on me father tape machine. De old man himself
just bob him head so, until *Zion Train* a come
on and him rise and begin fe skank, and me join

him, laughing and singing. Is so me develop de switch
that when me finally go lang and reach Babylon mek
some a de big islanders tek me for tone-down-Trini

and de small islanders tek me for book-bred Jamaican
and me play a lang, nyamming all de love of de community
cos inna dat Babylon cold, a hot dumpling pon stew chicken

was heaven, Zion in a sweet bun. Imagine now how
me surprise when me come and find that me name Parkes
is actually from a Jamaican ancestor, a returnee fe Sierra Leone

come as a soldier fe buffalo de locals into line fe de Babylon
system. But see it now: him arrive and see de way de yard
people dem shake dem batty and him desert, drop him uniform,

switch from brown to Maroon, and let de jungle suck him in;
no wonder that *Zion Train* can mek we rise still.

BACKGROUND

It had to be one of the zestful boys I played football with —
the cheeky one who made everyone smile. I liked him myself,
his forthright speech, considered him a good friend (still do).
I'm not quite sure how you chose him out of the ten, but I think
I know why — sure I was cheating with the Spanish girl, the one
who tended tomatoes — you let your heart bleed raw and unchecked.
I should have noticed your darkening moods, the curt lines, the chill
that crept into the current of our conversations, but I was still
bright-eyed enough to think that all clouds carry gifts of sun, happy
to wait for warmth. Besides, it was expected; your Italian blood boiled
swift as quicklime. It was only when I spied you kissing your way up
a hill that I knew our day was broken. It was the oddest awakening,
learning that I could hurt like a wound although I didn't love you.
I remember him coming — two days later — to ask me if I was fine
with him seeing my ex-girlfriend; I wasn't aware we had broken up.
Regardless, I nodded and began to play back collective evenings
out, lunches in the canteen, the way you slapped his arm, laughed
at his jokes, your eyes closing to slits, sharp as a dagger — tiny
incisions in the rooted grip of your affections but enough to plant
seeds. Now I get periodic jpegs of your two dark-eyed children
by e-mail — large files, with fields and fences picturesque
in the background. They have his unruly hair, in their mouths
his small teeth shine; there is always a measure of sun — no clouds —
and they hold hands, squinting into the light. I imagine you and he
on the other side of the camera, looking like you looked that day
I saw you wipe your red lips off his lower lip, the day I went home
wiser and stood by my open window, looking over Bedford fields
while the riddled curtain you loved to grasp danced like a ghost.

2

"History is not all that humankind possesses"
– Gao Xingjian

AYITEY, 1973

Portent in the air, always – a sense of change
coming – in Hanoi, Manila, in the ring
of pugilists. Our father, undoubtedly watching
that haze of fists and feet, must have felt a twinge,

some primordial premonition of his seed's skin flaming
in the kiln of his new wife, hardening in stance
as Marcos declares himself irreplaceable and George
Foreman, forearms like torpedoes, plants on Joe Frazier

the pin of defeat that Nixon couldn't fix on his map

of Vietnam. The end of your second trimester was
nothing short of dramatic, but your coming, two days
preceded by the first cellular phone call, a day after
the opening of the World Trade Center, brings more fire:

propane expands with a bang in Arizona, France flexes
mushroom clouds in Mururoa Atoll, aeroplanes crash
like toys and an energy crisis grips the West – this is to say
nothing of the fiery gleam of a saxophone going dim
in a pawnbroker's window, the abandoned music sheets

found years later turned yellow in a chest. There will be
better times – a spidery steel suspension, kin to another
that spans the Volta (the electric heart of Ghana), will reflect
its lights in the black waters between Asia and Europe, stitching

the space between two continents. Apart from the facts, I have

nothing to pit on the drama of your birth with; I've seen the date
list: in order – the birth of Sean Paul, Oscar De La Hoya; the death
of Pablo Picasso; Haile Gebrselassie (birth); the fall of Bruce Lee;
the first cry of Nasir Jones (also the son of a horn

player, later known as Nas) then this – in one line, poetry and a dearth
of poetry – Pablo Neruda leans into his own shadow, inherits
its weightlessness, fades with the night. It is September 23, 1973,
you are almost six months old. There is a picture of you sprawled
in an ocean of bed, a hard thing, a pin on a map, a wriggling spider

in a cream web, crying.

PEBBLES, 1980

Back then I was six, still learning to throw
grass spears, running headlong into the full
mysteries of Accra. Of course there were things
I would find out later: Richard Pryor catching fire

trying to freebase, the launch of *CNN*, the invention
of *Post-It* notes, the reason why my mother cried
out so loud that night at the end of January when
the rains came with no warning and left muddy waters

stagnant along the road to school. I recall I was

so in love with my English teacher that I wanted her
to be my mother, and I had learnt the national anthem
after the coup d'état the June before. It was the year
Ayitey and I learned about politics – with only one TV

channel we had no choice; crowded around the bright
orange box from *Philips*, we watched black and white
images of Zimbabwe gaining Independence. We were
so proud because Mugabe's wife was Ghanaian; it was our
victory. We juggled the sweetness of words like "struggle"

and "justice"; we could even pronounce *proletarians* – we were
joyous freedom fighters whose only moments of sadness came
at bedtime, and on the day Daddy said John Lennon was
shot. A year so full of drama we almost missed the swelling

of Mummy's belly, her widening nostrils, the slackening of

her pace and lowering of her heels. But who could forget
the kicks you dealt our ears in the months before you emerged
in October – so violent that Daddy chose to name you Pebbles
after Fred Flintstone's restless redhead daughter. Imagine that!

This was how you arrived three days before Margaret Thatcher
claimed "the lady's not for turning", your tough reputation
preceding you, crying out louder than Robert Mugabe,
your limbs all funny, jerky as a man on fire.

THE FALL, 1983

Had we known then what we know now,
we would never have tried, but back then
things like politics, physics, gravity, didn't

hold our attention. Everything was bright
to us; the sun so white in our eyes we believed
we were the only colour in the world.

Lebanon was in a shade of peace – stilled
from war – and regardless of what anyone said
about you, I had never heard a name so

beautiful: *Sajeeda*. Late afternoon, we held

hands by the gutter as we walked to our
secret haunt. Above the graveyard of cars,
our seven-year-old bodies twisted into

the rust and glass cage of a Nissan Sunny –
forsaken. Nested, we didn't consider the odds
of dropping like dislodged eggs. In that

strange skyscraper of scrap – a monument
to your mechanic father's failures, the precise
shape of the green tree in his flag – we

solemnly undressed, as one. We embraced

with the hope of nation builders,
founders of a club, only for our members
to tell us we were too young;

our bodies hadn't yet learnt
the temperature of knowledge,
the fitting moment to harden

for confrontation, or when
to lower the flag, yield
to break the fall of a heart.

THE RAINY SEASON, 1984

Those specious days, when we sucked on sweets
for so long that the roofs of our mouths burned raw
as fired kilns, our friendship firmed, shaped
on lathes of incessant dares. I am thinking
about that rainy season when everything changed;

when we stared into violent currents of rainwater
gushing downhill in the open, roadside drainage – fat

with the harvest of North Kaneshie's pungent excess –
and Kofi, undeterred by the dark, swirling depths,

leapt across the gutter leaving us glaring, stumped
on the side of caution; when mangoes were so swollen
with sun we forgot about the drought of the year
before; when I trailed my big brother to school
early, to watch him squeeze the budding breasts

of older girls into permanence; when Osei returned
early from school to find some man calming the fire
of his mother's famine, raising his head – saurian –

to suck on humid air.

THE FALL OF MAN
Genesis 3: 19

in the sweat of thy face

As dew settled, a weightless membrane on the morning's
colour, he stood three floors up – visible only to those
who would lift their eyes to heaven. The image he offered
was patterned by the lattice of a balcony wall – a slow-moving
thing, like a beetle lugging its world across a tree's shadow.
Omnipresent, he was there when we swept away the previous
day's secrets, its discarded veil of orange, fractured green
and dust; there when we emerged soap-sanctified, books
heavy in our arms, foreheads gleaming like polished copper,
to wind our mischievous way to school; he was there, dripping
sweat, when we returned, his speech louder but unchanged
– a thurible of monotone mumbles, hissing now and then
when doused by a splash of clarity.

shalt thou eat bread

At four pm, predictable as a lizard's nod, he'd go indoors
and cook for his children – Ato and Yaa – the boy with a scar
the shape of a leaf, and the girl with wild brown curls forever
anchored with a thin yellow headband. The duo kept his money
in ever-shifting hiding places to save him from the man he had
become. But if you stayed in the dappled stencil of a mango
tree's shade, daydreaming while nibbling fruit or burnt
toast until all form seeped into darkness, you'd see him
re-emerge, lay the timber of his forearms on the balcony's wall
and shudder.   There is no name for the sensation
a child feels watching a giant cry. We only knew him as Barima,
which translates (weakly) to *man* in English, making him more
slippery than fine spun silk, the mysteries of his grief giving
seed to the myriad stories that flourished in the valley of our youth.

till thou return unto the ground
My siblings fed on the most colourful: the resurrection theory
that went like this: once, thirteen years before we knew him,
an Englishman disappeared from a life in London so that his wife
could collect an insurance payout for losing him. He came back
to life in the birthplace of his wife and mother, only to hear his beloved
had taken ill. Months later, his *orphaned* children – one and two – are
shipped to their closest living kin, his mother-in-law, who delivers
the children, but not the wealth she inherited, leaving him heartbroken
etcetera etc. There were sixteen such stories. My concerns were
in the present (now past): every night, subject to the unpredictable
threat of falling mangoes, I watched him sip and sway in the night's
wind, his thickening waist visible above the balcony wall's lip, wondering
when he would lose his balance, tip and tumble from his tower.

WINGS, 1987

Whatever it was that stopped me from joining,
I can't deny that I was fascinated by it: cadet
corps — all drills, shrill commands, shining

boots, whistles and caps. The guns were kept
in a rectangular building with a flat roof, in front
of which the recruits would march, crunching gravel

with their swift about-turns and halts. One
of the best armouries in the country I was told —
Why do you think the campus is called Outlaw's Hill?

At night, the structure was lit by a single
stuttering, fluorescent light, a halo that framed
its width and the notorious level of its height —

the roof from which my father and brother jumped
as part of their training, triumphs described
in the sonorous tones of exclusivity. I wanted

to own that history, feel my legs folding beneath
me to break my fall. It was forbidden; prefects
kept a watchful eye, ready to catch rebels —

boys and girls who chose to test their mettle
against gravity. But, once I got the idea, nothing
could stop me. I remember the lift from the balls

of my feet, the quick swat of air on my face
and then a pause, an emptiness in which I hovered
between fear of death, and fear of discovery

if I survived. Both fears diminished in mid-air
as I felt the transient exhilaration of flight, forgetting
the crunch of hard gravel, the earth coming at me fast.

THE CUT

I

We could be seen from the air, I'm sure,
but who would dare fly so close to the sun
when even the earth felt like a lick of fire?
A day when the benign insane, abandoned

to wander in circles as tangled as their hair,
knew not to emerge from the shade. Determined,
we sweated in the glare, consuming the quota
of shallow breaths required to get us to the bend

where, briefly, tall elephant grass would alter
its heavenward path to embrace us and weave us
into the weeds and wildlife that thrived by the rail line –
fertile ground for many reasons. Home to (as

rumour had it) a thriving hub of con men, blind
killers – society's scum whose shit lent crass
fecundity to the crunchy, top layer of fine,
many storeyed dust. Trains still occasionally cast

their restless shadows over the tracks, but there had been
no timetable for years – no thought for the likes of us.

II

We had no business there, yet there we were,
clad in cloned blue shorts. Nine and ten, we knew
right from wrong but couldn't fight the lure. Undercover
conversations (the same that told of a man or two

lurking out there who could accelerate a life – whatever
it was – negatively or positively) had assured us
that this legendary short cut would get us to Circle in under
nine minutes. We planned our trip to our grandparents'

in Adabraka – a five minute jaunt from Circle – with care,
in low tones, passed notes. Of course, we didn't think of the grapevine –
the neighbours that saw us creeping out, the direct Grandpa-
to-Daddy phone line. So there we were, our thin

legs rickety as our breaths when we turned limber
to avoid a choking train, our chests tight from the anticipation
of meeting our deaths at the hands of some roving murderer.
So tense with shivers we didn't notice – beneath our

sandals – the source of the stench, the accusing fingers
that followed us like a swarm of curses to Adabraka.

III

There is history, naturally. The rail tracks were laid
to run to the port, carrying raw materials to new
destinies. The docks were the point of entry for trade-
goods and the Sierra Leonean grandfather we never knew

who was a disciplinarian famed for his skill
and ferocity with leather belts – a skill Daddy had
inherited but used with more restraint and less of the devil.
There is context, too. Our mother, who saw to it that we prayed

at night, had been away for months – we hadn't gone wild
but there was no religion in our lives. And this is how the story ends:
Grandpa – home alone – receives us. We lie, (with style
and poise) about how we got there but can't explain

the smell of our feet. He calls our father and gives us enough
money to take a taxi back home. We opt to spend it on roast plantain
and groundnuts, skipping the free ride to quaff
the sweet blackened-yellow subs and savour the dampened refrain

of the finest *Arachis hypogaea* in Africa as we tackle the rail line again —
to combat and cure the jitters of the first time. We arrive home, brown
with caked sand, shower and put ourselves to bed at 3pm, hoping
morning will come soon. We discover insomnia. Then, slow

as fate, comes the sound of Daddy's key in the lock, then
hours of wily silence. At 7pm we hear him knock at our door;
unsure whether to be awake or asleep, we bury our heads
in the quicksand of our bed sheets and pray.

JERRY, 1999

We inherited the stick and the position –

whenever the team was struggling and needed
pace and guile, the ball was struck hard
towards the right wing into open space

and, if the white orb was slower than light,

chances were my brothers or I would stop it,
feint to the left, prod the ball right
and take off, blurring like lost years

while we merged with the dust of Achimota School,

headed for the scoring circle, our hockey sticks
flashing occasionally like swords or light sabres.
In that moment we were all called Jerry;

our father's name bolted from the coach's lips,

excited and insistent. It didn't matter
whether it was 1987, 1988 or 1999
when my younger brother played. For Mr. Asare,

who used to pass the ball to my father in 1960,

our speed and passion was a legacy,
our cheeky smiles after scoring
something only a father could pass on.

BY YOURSELF, BOY… (1988 – 2007)

Q1

The basketball games I used to watch were
taped from a scrambled channel, had no sound
to speak of. I used to replay them in my head,
lend my own fillip to the images, splice them

into details: a hand like the arc of a mother's
belly awaiting the return of a ball sent down
to concrete; a half-raised foot – pre-fake and swivel;
a fall, fluid and dramatic, alive with the sweat

of exertion. For me, the moves had no names
but there were patterns in the chaos; determination
flexed hard on five faces usually muscled a win.

Q2

Those games had a silent energy that hung over
me, left clouds in my head that school could not
disperse. Walking past the main court for my piano
lessons, I would stop, listen to the older boys bragging,

belittling each other as they contorted their bodies
into screens of guile. I only went four times before
I skipped my first lesson – enough time for me to learn
scales, how to hold my hand above the keys, curved

like a basketball, but not enough to play anything
but *do re mi* and the bass lines of hit songs I'd heard
at the time. It seemed like music had lost the battle.

Q3

I learnt the language of the court: how to bow
low to breeze beyond the barriers of the zone,
crack my opponents by calling them names, advising
them to go home, spend some time alone learning

the rudiments of the game. This became my music —
the trash talk notated with polyrhythms of bounce,
the *oohs* and *ahhs*, the slick refrain of a swish shot.
I saw no connection between my new world and the one

I had deserted — the high post of the piano's back
the timed tap of feet, the bounce of hammers responding
to fingers and wires — until nineteen years later.

Q4

Nat King Cole's on the TV staring hard at his audience,
his hands setting up plays while he sings. Ray Charles
said he sang so damn well people forgot how good he was
on keys, and I see it now: his right hand stuffs a melody

down the grand piano's throat — that's the fake — he dribbles
the sound down to low notes until you expect the left hand
to come in lower. That's when he breaks mould, hustles
his left hand over the right, throws high notes into your ear

— crossover, up, swish. Now the trash talk *it's better to be
by yourself boy* ... He smiles like the silent men on my tapes
and, suddenly, every move has a name, a sound, a history.

STRIPPING YAM

There was always us; two boys staking out
the kitchen as territory to invade;
new smells of the land born into us, a magnet

to the warm centre that made us
dark. We discovered a new vocabulary for hunger –
abele ni a sha, karklo, kelewele

and yɛlɛ ni a sha, yɛlɛ kɛ kontomire, yɛlɛ ni a shi
always yɛlɛ. We fell in love
with yam in its different guises, always beguiling.

We fell in love without knowing
its history, appreciating its journey from village
farm to town compound, without

reaching into the breast of earth to feel it swell
from chunk to tuber; we were
enamoured without the encircling of yam's green

vines begging for attention; ours
was a love divorced from the past, a love inspired
by the dark, tough skin we knew

held fibre that could render us silent so our jaws
could move. Yɛlɛ, a name that
reconfigured our nervous systems, linked our ears

so intimately to our tongues
that the sound of frying yams made our hunger blues
switch to wet, red-pink

like litmus; we were so rooted to present joys till
1983 brought dry Sahel winds
and turned the word yɛlɛ to whispers – *yɛlɛ, yɛlɛ* –

so difficult to find, so tough
to conjure when the soil's fertility was compromised
and there was us, two boys

learning to live on a meal-a-day and the memory
of the sound of frying yams.
We became like yams – hard and dark as mango

tree bark in the relentless sun,
smiling at each other, remembering past Aprils
when kindred birthdays gave

license to our family to cook and mash yams. Ot<u>o</u>
made by communal effort. Us
two boys cutting and stripping yams of darkness,

our mother washing the slices
and putting them in the pot till they emerged soft
to be mashed by our father then

mixed with spiced palm oil until a red mountain
topped with eggs – boiled, shelled
white – declared that we were a year older; there

was always us; two boys sitting
around a plate, eating, dreaming, talking, growing
suffering together. And, like yams

the harder we are beaten, the stronger we bond; stick
to our purpose as fufu does
to fingers, so there is always us, two boys becoming

men. So each time I buy yams
their stripping becomes the telling of the story
of us, two boys, two men

hiding the fibre beneath our skins with smiles
and the sizzling sound of frying
yams is always ours; the sound of sweet struggle.

3

"We have had to ask but little of imagination… our crucial problem has been a lack of conventional means to render our lives believable."

— Gabriel Garcia Marquez

THE BALLAST SERIES

Bright ball of flame that thro the gloom of even
Silently takest thine ethereal way
And with surpassing glory dimmst each ray
Twinkling amid the dark blue depths of Heaven

— Percy Bysshe Shelley
(from "To a Balloon Laden with Knowledge")

BALLAST I: A GENEROUS COURIER

The lot distils to a case
of bad synchronisation,

the drip-slow appreciation
of fire, its taming, and uses.

What with round-the-world
sponsored balloon flights

insured by the same companies
that insured the heavy cargo

of seventeenth to nineteenth
century Atlantic trading ships,

and the 19th century theory
that eked men out of fishes —

in Patagonia? — it strikes me
empirically, the same way

moon strikes night and sun day,
that I would have wings by now;

for if the triangle was serviced
by balloon, and the debate had

arisen when matters reached a low
point, between sugar and slaves

for use as ballast, crows would
be fluent in Yoruba and Mende,

Hausa and Akan, and *Ebonics*
still would be the sound of thunder.

BALLAST II: THE BIRTH OF LIQUID DESIRES

Our planked fathers drowned simply
because weight is whatever we keep inside.

Within the coffin confines
of blood-lined breathing space

they inhaled death and hate,
extracted pride, then exhaled hope.

And the same way balloonists
couldn't contain within paper and silk

the fiery resolve of burning straw,
cast iron couldn't collar their spirits.

Protest songs swelled blue within them
as they willed themselves to die

to spite the traders. Profit demanded
unnatural solutions to recover from Aetna

and Lloyds the potential gains
of defiant pre-cadaver bodies,

so the weight of pride was heft and thrown
overboard. Swollen, they dropped, though

balloon men flew – soon after, in Paris,
1783 – and the farmers didn't like it,

but grew joyous when offered champagne –
bottles that popped like drowned corpses

and sang the songs that had fermented
inside them all those frustrating years.

BALLAST III: TURTLE IN THE SKY WITH FIRE IN ITS LUNGS

It probably never registered, even
after the advent of balloons,

that vertical velocity increases
when you drop weight. The focus

no doubt remained on keeping
the slave trade aloft after 1783

when slave ships experienced a curious
legal falling from grace, negative upright

thrust, because the *Zong* tossed slaves
overboard in a quest for profits.

Faced with ruin for fraud, I wonder
if the ship's Liverpool owners looked

to the sky and contemplated
the possibilities of balloon transport;

how men offloaded from high
enough just might attain the right

speed to make the transition
from nuisance to pure light,

having outstripped their screams,
history and whatever units Einstein

might have been able to measure;
how the energy that built the West

might have transformed from darkness
into random shafts of lightning.

BALLAST IV: FLUNG OUT LIKE A FAG-END

The ships that sank never really stood
a chance; the captured in the holds, less.

In water, gravity numbed at the cost of oxygen
made their breaths catch for a taste

of weightlessness – space, centuries before
the Buzz became news. Odd, how we explore

the high and deep, rarely the middle – that belt
of rarefied air which balloons occupy, where

the cargo would have avoided the brutal fury
of waves. Battered, at worst, by hurricanes, there

was still the likelihood of a short period of calm
at the axis – a respite from evil winds – before

the centrifugal drag of the eye wall: a flutter of
freed bodies floating to the ends of the world

to feather new nests, a basket falling, an envelope
drifting, a fire augmenting the speed of migration

from Africa beyond a fast-fingered jazz solo, minus
the 500 years of insult: in the bodies, fire;

in the basket, gifts; in the envelope, odds on whether
the seeds of the scattered would have avoided Katrina

– the dancing wind that exposed the unchanging water
-borne illness of prejudice caught in the holds of

ships that made it across the sky's reflection two
centuries before the eerie shimmer of a hot air balloon.

BALLAST V: THE PERSISTENCE OF MEMORY

Cast as mushrooms, their elevation
anchored to conditions of shifting

winds, temperature and the expertise
of their cloud-hued captains, these

vessels would have borne their cargo
away, home bright in the distance,

fading. Indeed, the forced labour
still may have prevailed – families

shackled to impossible demands
of plantation owners. However, one

might decode the flexed helix of how
the persistence of memory informed

the shaping of cheeks as domes akin
to a balloon's envelope. How kindred

fire within a Dizzy one could produce
the height of ecstasy from sound, how,

refused goggles for the hue of their eyes,
Wonders were blinded by altitude, yet

retained enough wind to sing of sunshine
generations later. Quite simply, genetic

memory made metaphor, musical time
stretched like currents, songs escaping

to ribbon the sky – like a whipped hem
of waves laying claim to the shore.

Then comes the moment: a woman,
bent over her baby and a white ball

of balloon cotton en route to a basket,
slides from the sun-burnt present

into the inner-world of winged instinct
— the museum of genius and fancy.

Here she encounters her airborne
self, aloft above the fruitful trinity

of Africa, Europe and the Americas,
knowing instantly that it is better

to be light, else be cast out, sacked,
because downsizing is called for

to ensure maximum gain. Genius
informs her that all emotions must

be suppressed to stanch care's blood,
for love is a wound here, a tool

that can be used to tighten chains,
restrict breathing for the greater ease

of lightness. The moment passes
away; the woman out — and the baby is

saved by the basket. No drums to lead
her spirit back home, so work songs are

hummed — a zing inhabits the air like a gin
and a cotton cloud floats away, orphaned.

BALLAST VII: STEPS

The first few would pass, barely
upheld by a mild-tempered wind,

heavy as sin darkening the earth
briefly – like a flash of anger

in the eyes of a mother. Oval spectres,
they would leave skies plastered

with maps for lost followers. The next
couple would mass like a washerwoman's

fists dripping opaque secrets to parachute
into the arms of truth, a semination

of sorrow. In the year of the *Zee*
the vessels would balloon in number,

choking the sky with their cumulus
as they drifted above the Atlantic's blue

ink in a pattern scrawled to feed
the stubborn viscosity of a treacle dream.

Assembled, they'd hover close to the music
of cane falling, to the rhythm of cotton-

picking, poised over pocketed land, loaded
with the saliva of Thunder's ranting. This

is where the pale science would begin, the miraculous
steps leading from massed clouds to rich harvest;

the dissection of families into working slivers,
the seeds of a storm that haunts the skies still.

BALLAST VIII: PEPPER

Helpless to stop the occasional loss of vessels
to the vicissitudes of chance and bird strikes,

survivors would note the sound of escape
the air made – a *whoosh* that called every man,

woman and child to notice. Then, strapping memories
of intangible flavours to their thighs, they spread

out, their shackles pealing like wind chimes, borderless
as they fan like open hands, moths, to new lands.

On arrival, each falls upon the earth, famished, clamouring
for the pig and pepper, the bean and salt of home;

whatever pulse, flesh or spice they find, they adapt – *ackee*
for eggs, salt-fish for *dide,* chickpeas for black beans and potatoes

for sweeter roots. How they would celebrate to find home
in the soil! *Malanga* and *yucca* for cocoyam and *manioc,*

the *cebolla* of *sabolai* – losing their tongues in the salted
ecstasy of carnival, forgetting that salt would anchor their feet

in exile, steal the languages behind their teeth, leaving
whiteness – though previous arguments would persist in the music

and manner of speaking. Never fading would be the sounds of the drum
sequences reproduced on the stretched skins of beasts they had

seasoned with bark and bay leaves; the wings of large birds,
flapping before those ominous chirps – signalling anger, impatience –

and that haunting hiss of air escaping, to be mimicked later
with tooth and tongue, cutting through crowds like a winged curse.

BALLAST IX: POOL

It is true there were kidnappings, dark-
skinned posses in the dead of night claiming

victims of similar hue. And we've condemned
those raiders for making commodities of men

who were their *brothers*. Now, with flying vessels,
the advantages from the home-angle would be:

having the loading done on land, the elite squad – kings'
men – would be close enough to hear the chatter projecting

from the mouths of their commissioners, eliciting,
by observing the twists of lips, filtering the highs

and lows, licks and grunts, winks and tones
of smile, that these travellers spoke not the same

brand of deceit, that they profited by continental gall,
forged their bond over the inherited pallor of their faces

– not the similarity of their tongues, walks or rituals.
Suddenly attuned to the change of rules, the fact

that these fraternal-acting traders of shifty eyes
and aspect had branded them kin to their strange

booty, our co-dark brothers would catch the panicked
pitch of captives crying foul before flight could reach

the height of no return. With the blimp's trailing rope
held still in a pool of tears, the chance would yet exist

to grab that fast-rising umbilicus, to correct errors,
re-*birth* our axis of fraternity – tie it to blackness.

BALLAST X: FINAL CRIES

If the river cries blood, it is not the sun's
reflection rosy beneath a retiring light, it is

not riverside berries, betrayed by skins too gorged
to contain the sweetness of their juice. It is not

a dream. It is our forebears, battered and branded by gain-
seekers, dripping iron, rusting, as they hover tethered

in baskets strung to sun-shaped fabrics that consume
fire to rise above the desire for freedom. Their voices –

like them – know nothing of the borders to come, slip
between clouds to metamorphose into birdsong. They

inhabit the air, absorb its language by osmosis, observe
its scattering versatility – the way it hisses and dances.

Some escape, diving into the spaces where hurricanes are
sown, to learn the equations that govern pressure; learn how

the cold air is enough to make them pop like champagne
bottles on ice. The fliers bequeath the inheritance of falling

gracefully; a blessing for dancers, a curse in love. Yet
in the end the method matters little. The sea being mirror

to the blue of the skies, the ship is the genetic cousin
of the balloon – both anchored to the Xs of density,

surface area and flotation. The question is of ballast,
that which gives weight to the ship, balloon, story, and this

interpretation is a vessel to reclaim the history of love, a history
of hatred, discrimination, survival, science, music… language.

4

"I grew up in this town, my poetry was born between the hill and the river, it took its voice from the rain, and like the timber, it steeped itself in the forests."

— Pablo Neruda

DRAUGHTS, EPHEMERA, FACTIONS…

i: *draughts*

Beside a gutter, a suspension
of dust and flies a foot above
an average man's head. Beneath it,
two benches, sometimes stools (the sort
we had in kitchens, worn smooth
and stained dark by sittings, conversations)
opposite each other, separated by a square
of squares, a draughts board. It is
the mysteries of this you took me to
discover after Marvin Gaye died
and you found me crying. I was struck
by the machine-gun speed of rounds
and squares slapping the two-toned
wood, but, with time, you taught me
to observe the moves, analyse, slow
the sequence by thinking ahead, sizing
up my opponents, taking mental notes.

ii: *ephemera*

When a young Steve Grossman stood
in for Wayne Shorter at Miles Davis's
Fillimore East gig, you took note. That
gig was recorded and released, of course,
but you catalogued many more: live sessions
you saw in London, variations in chord
changes on recordings of the same song,
majestic solos by Bird, Mingus, Peterson,
Coleman… You may have sold your tenor
saxophone for fatherhood, but you never stopped

grazing in the jazz grass. Then there are
the outlines for stories, one-legged poems
that waited 2½ decades for you to complete;
I saved them from being discarded after
you died, sorted them into short stories, poems,
novel ideas, kept letters that help almost make
sense of our blown dandelion family...

iii: *factions*

I remember the clandestine
arrivals, half-sisters and brothers,
changing colour like chameleons with
the shifting hues of early early morning,
bearing on their chattering lips, reasons
why you could no longer trust red-
eyed (who had been there the morning before),
how yellow-belly had insulted them. You
would listen, dredge up a joke from the past,
get them laughing, then offer them a drink,
bundle them back out. You never got involved,
stayed on the periphery, welcoming all factions
silently, listening, taking notes. I wonder
if you filed those observations somewhere
in the kinks of your grey, beneath the sound
of slapped draughts, jazz solos, stories
whispering their skeletons to a future alive.

CIRCUS

Some afternoons I wonder about the girl or
man, centuries from now – another genus?–
who will excavate in our wake, seeking clues
in the riddled limestone of our passing
about how we lived – the mysteries of our blue
nights, the deviations that laced our days.

Not wise to our age of ships, crossed borders,
they'll dig beneath a Japanese maple gone
native in a European city where I lived,
slave to its fire and scent and song,
where I bloomed on alcohol and fractured ice
and my love coaxed meals from chance and spice.

Right there, where they'll linger with axes,
we danced as joint and socket in the honey
of dusk, months before we settled (with child)
in the bosom of the city's hills, years prior
to the coming of the circus, its tusked ivory,
its hypermobile performers, its masters of enterology –
the lights, the decorated bedlam, the skilled
weaving of magic into every moment
burnished that returning circus into myth.
Little wonder then, that the contortionist was,
on dying, mourned wide and kept folded – as
found – boxed and buried where he drew applause.

Right there. And after him came the market's chaos:
weekends of fish and bread and basil,
then the arboretum – all variegated petals
and palmate leaves, awash with the smell of citrus
and birdsong – that fell into disuse the fall
after its sponsor died, growing unkempt, spreading wild.

Water ran through it once, where the earth will meet the axe;
layer by layer, with academic focus, they'll sift past
the musk of our dancing nights, past the basil and birds,
beyond the roots of the wild maple and strike a box
no higher than their knees and find within a body pleated,
distilled to a fallen-Jenga of bones, unrattled by its rebirth

as the spirit, the epitome of Homo sapiens sapiens.

WHAT I KNOW

This is what I know; that I wake
up one morning when I am eight and walk
outside to the sound of a cock crowing.
The leaves on the first tree I touch are black
and gleam with whispers from the night's passing.
All about me are shadows and I am, at once,

unsure of what I know: the bushes I kicked
my ball past yesterday are pumped with new muscles
and rise from the riddled haze in front of me
as sentinels from another realm. The cock has gone
quiet and I curse myself for stepping unshod
into the moist mystery afoot at the calling of a phantom

cock. I blink three times but the shroud will not peter
and, behind me, footsteps echo like a call to the sun.
When my father reaches me I raise my arm and point
in front of me: what is that? *Mist*, he replies –
and what do I know of mist, its shifting brilliance, its weightless
weight, its liquid kiss? But I know the shape I pointed at,

my love, that brooding morning
under my father's darkness, and tonight
I name you – you are mist.

MEN LIKE ME

My mother warned me about laid-back men
like me. Men with lazy leans and sharp eyes,
who love nothing better than an evening
on a street corner tasting the world, slice

by sour slice. Men with rough beards and dreadlocks,
whose hands are comfortable settling into
pockets. Men with a thousand ways to pause
and paint plain days in shades of awe and blue,

who dream in many dialects, smell of spice,
men whose tongues slide easily over lips.
My mother told me to steer clear of wise-
cracking men like me, sun-hardened, with deep

laughs and tattoos, usurping God's calling
as creator, rewriting their own skins.

FAITH

It looked like a landing strip – long corridor of concrete –
rectangular, yet composed of square slabs; granted,
it was nobody's idea of the centre of excellence it was –
that grey platform muttering with our reluctant footsteps

at 5 a.m., with sleep still scratching at the eyes of the gathered.
From there, we were sent on our four kilometre morning
run, a housemaster waiting with a stopwatch for our return.
But come afternoon, in the wake of siesta, the sun still

harsh above the sandy horizon, ants trailblazing coded patterns
on the edges of the hot stone slabs, we assembled willingly
to live out our dreams. To the left, some triple-jumped
into a world of wild flowers – reds, purples and yellows

blazing beneath their petalled limbs; sprinters exploded
from end to end; footballers juggled and dribbled; while
devotees of the orange bounce – the most recent Michael Jordan-
inspired craze – faked invisible opponents into embarrassing falls.

In the midst of all that, this snapshot: diffused light cannoning
off dust towards the eye, an ethereal tint framing the impossible
profusion of stilled energy – the tamarind tree green in leaf
and ideal for perspective – and in the foreground, me. I am

attempting my first ever back flip. Barefoot, I have flexed
my feet, felt my calves and thighs twitch and engage, swung
my arms fifteen degrees backwards, then suddenly forwards
as I take off, not knowing which part of my body will lead

the renewal of my contact with the ground. There is no mattress,
no coach – just my biology and the concrete. This is how
the camera catches me – suspended in an act of faith, my
back arched instinctively, arms searching the air behind me,

my body drawing a taut line beneath the question:
Do you believe in that which you can not see?

DAY DREAMING

In a world where the sun rises for me, lights
peer from cracks in the roof
and a stag is spooked, paralysed by the concrete

spectre of a man, legless,
watching. Through glass, dark, in the distance,
I see a horse hung in mid-air;

one of many figures arrested, caught living, but gone
still – stiff as the dead; a bird
floating above a pear-like flame; a midget cornered

in pastel; four elements
in gold frames. Echoes multiply and fade, marking
my passage, reminiscent

of the sound in the black-and-white tiled hall where
my hesitant steps first
marked a slow entry into independence, the hard

cell of responsibility –
Achimota School. Here I learned the components
of light, the taste of fear,

sculpture's stiff pride, the chemistry of paint,
and I found a bright sun
doesn't always mean a good day for dreaming.

DINNER FOR ONE

The smell of onions punctuates the void
that swallows my rage. I'm hoping
you heard the click when I smashed my phone

against the wall. My breath returns
with the rhythm of indignation
underlined by swift stabs of remorse.

Maybe I shouldn't have been so
damned stubborn. I stir the blue
pan of onions and herbs, suddenly

aware that I will be eating alone.
Outside the sky turns a neutral
rain-fat grey with cotton shapes

shifting at the level speed of climate
change. I call out your name in the yellow
square of my bedsit, switch off the red-hot

hob and head outside. The air
swallows my spice-tinged skin and offers me
moisture and a hint of metal.

INTERJECTION

Transport is lateral ageing, and motion triggers
what is mere steam: memory, moments,

the time I spent sandwiching the soft
bellies of my poems between the frantic

shrieks of trains passing, learning the rhythm
of the stop lights – the way they controlled

pitch, speed, volume and frequency
like a voice box; the audience watching

me, listening to my renderings of another
place – an age prior – while I fine-tuned

my pauses and filled them with smiles;
across the room a camera freezing me like

a red light, and, later, me learning the room
I read in, used to be the Bethel, Connecticut

station – a place of changes, interjections –
and, though it was a distant memory, the trains

that passed through ran on steam. And why
I remember this now, on a train, my hands

wrapped around a cardboard cup of steaming
cocoa halfway to my lips, just as I was thinking

of how I used to be an alto when I was younger
– not this stop-start tenor-bass – is anyone's guess.

INCLINATION

I have come too far for an easy return,
invested my trust in rugged wheels and a six-
fingered man. There are five of us – and our
weight deepens the severity of our challenge.
We are in a ditch, all angles and flimsy traction,
mud flying with each rev. Yet it is not
the splashes that trouble me, not the creak
of metal straining to hold its shape; I am
contemplating balance. I am recalling
a mottled green bench in my school yard,
North Kaneshie, Accra, my rear end snug
on its edge, laughter resonant in the post-
snack-break chatter, until my four friends rise
as one – and I fall, the bench rises like the hull
of a torpedoed ship to strike me: five
minus four *equals* fall. And here, engine
rumbling beneath me, I revert to mathematics,
the formulae of lees. Will horsepower *minus* human
weight *plus* driver skill heave us up this hill? Will
my companions scramble, leaving me to the whims
of gravity? Whose thin wisp of a voice is reciting Psalm
23? *Thy rod and thy staff they comfort me...*

THE SNAKE'S REVENGE

In the natural order of things
the mamba's fangs would have won
the colourless tug of breath lying down.

But my father defied reason. Centuries
of fine-tuning,
of fang-sharpness, depth

and angle of approach
for the right poisonous

resonance, held no music
for his feet to dance.
He realigned balance.

Venom carefully distilled
by a stone-cold
man-killing process,

to tantalise, mesmerise
and render lifeless, barely
unsettled his wide stride.

Sunrise came and he rose
whistling like a bird,

mocking the mamba green,
his walk a straight insult,
his smile a curved expletive,

an invertebrate taunt
responded to silently
with sibilant spite:

a circulating curse
buried beneath the span

of his skin like tobacco
tucked within thin paper

awaiting a spark to speak
smoke messages to a transient heaven
and leave grey clues for slow, evil

cancerous spirits that would haunt
the hollows of my father's blood vessels –
whispering genies awaiting release.

A FAMILIAR VOICE AT THE V&A MUSEUM

The music of my footsteps shadows me
in the high ceiling of the entry hall.
I remember the movement being louder,
delivered with greater forte
by the staccato
                    fingers of my infant legs.

Down the hall the enchantment remains,
but the awe of my flitting eyes is gone;
for in my journey, tales of the supernatural
have become natural, so I see the battles,
the blood, the women wooed, the men
double-crossed for a runaway place in
history that ripples in ever widening circles.

Yet nothing changes; each shiny surface
reflects the same me – alone this time –
taller, but bearing fossilised gestures,
hearing the Morse code of high heels
criss-crossing over a carbon cacophony
twenty-four years earlier – faint but surefooted
alongside the voices trapped in these walls like relics.

I can even hear my father's speech, bowel-
transmitted and comforting, obeying
the laws of physics – fading infinitesimally
but never dying – in this place he showed me;
joining the thunderous chorus of the dead
and living that only griots applaud; labelled insane
because they have found the logic of science.

So historians change everything,
remould the stories of this museum
to fit the code of the day as the previous
conjurers become fodder for plants
and nature wins. For flora script history better than men –
unhindered by prejudice, inspired only by an insatiable
desire for sunlight.

Nothing changes after all, though surfaces
are polished daily; these swords, shields
bowls and manuscripts are but matter
moved and moulded, and this hall
is the same, although I have lost
the warmth of a hand and the colour
of my father's speech to history.

REBELLION

Alright, mother, I admit it! Sometimes rebellion was
a sour drop on my tongue – I was so enamoured
of its aftertaste I had to have more. Those late hours
when I was silent, my mouth was a zoo – a horde

of secret creatures
                    leaping from cheek to cheek.
Yet thinking about it now, I wonder if you observed
them flashing across my eyes – scatting their mystique,
their graceful steps – a cat's gaze narrowing my lids

before I fell asleep. I hope you will forgive my
suspicion that you stealthily let me savour
little victories so my lips would be sealed by

the slow melt of discretion – because no matter
how often I replay those serpentine hours, divine
for truth, I can't seem to erase your knowing smile.

THE PRINCESS AND THE PEA

The clouds outside are heavy and shaped
like humps; inside there are two –
a man and a woman – caught in a moment
of arched backs. There is sorrow and the sound

of tears. She, with the wet cheeks, is the one
who is joyful, while he who wipes them is sad,
for he has forgotten how to cry when happy.
Maybe he never learned. This is the story

of the princess and the pea, except
there is no pile of mattresses to lie on.
He has planted a pea inside his beloved
and wonders if she'll ever know a tranquil

night again; but it took many days for a smile
to reach her and sleep is the last thing on her mind.
Is this not how families are built – on smiles
and the undulating sound of tears?

FADING TO WILD

Outside my window it is post-storm; grey-black
clouds have faded silver. A fresh peace hovers,

seeks crevices in which to plant its seeds;
my body yields nothing, packed hard

as parched clay, inhospitable. Metropolitan trees,
hesitant after the chaos, huddle beside lamps,

reach out their green tips, shivering in anticipation
of new breeze. Should they come, the winds

will find me still, with fists attempting to hold
onto whispers, a torso that has learned the rigid language

of trees, lips shaped to hold rage prisoner
and eyes that have squinted through the fierce

ball of elements, to see everything
as beautiful – except beauty itself.

It's the sirens again. I lean against the window-
frame and look outside to catch the fading

sapphires of law enforcement, big city graffiti
of coloured lights spread beyond the range of the eye;

for every light there is a sound – a kick, a crash,
a falling garbage can, the wild trainers of young

feet pounding the city into new shapes, leaving marks.
Distress cries lose their urgency in the frantic

shrieks of girls jubilating over new shoes, a kiss, some
tasty gossip. The pane reflects me and I look

into the eyes of a boy who grew up barefoot, soles
intimate with the curve of the earth's breast, cutting

through brush with chances of snake bites underfoot.
The forest envelopes me, climbers dampen

the city's quivering paranoia, the sirens fade to an owl's cry.

ABOUT THE AUTHOR

Nii Ayikwei Parkes is an author and performance poet who has performed on major stages across the world, including at The Royal Festival Hall and at a reading for the London Mayor's vigil on July 14, 2005 (in response to the London bombings). He is the author of the poetry chapbooks: *eyes of a boy, lips of a man* (1999), *M is for Madrigal* (2004), a selection of seven jazz poems and *Ballast* (2009), an imagination of the slave trade by balloon. His poem, "Tin Roof", was selected for the "Poems on the Underground" initiative in 2007 and his novel, *Tail of the Blue Bird* (Jonathan Cape, 2009) has been hailed by the *Financial Times* as "a beautifully written fable... simple in form, but grappling with urgent issues." Nii is the Senior Editor at flipped eye publishing, a contributing editor to *The Liberal*, a former poet in residence at The Poetry Café, a 2005 associate writer in residence on BBC Radio 3, and has held visiting positions at the University of Southampton and California State University.

As a socio-cultural commentator and advocate for African writing, Nii has led forums internationally, has sat on discussion panels for BBC Radio with literary heavyweights such as Booker winners, Margaret Atwood and A.S. Byatt, and he runs the African Writers' Evening series, at the Poetry Café in Covent Garden.

In 2007 he was awarded Ghana's National ACRAG award for poetry and literary advocacy.

6, April 2010; £8.99

between worlds: the familiar culture of
poet-speaker feels ambivalent towards,
earning, the "luminous sea of myth" that
ut of because of physical and intellectual
urney takes him away from home and into
learning, there comes a new vision of what
— a vision that can be represented through
rary imagination.

ellous book of generous, giving poems. Not only
on travel through an abiding language and far-
y, but it also transports the reader to a complex
errain through a basic honesty and truthfulness. The
of borders is executed with an ease that never fails to
ader's mind and body. There's a playfulness here that's
and, at times, even outrageous in its breathless insinua-
gh a biting clarity and directness that would have chal-
e Great Sparrow. Hutchinson is a young poet who seems
ey wherever his poems take him, and the reader is blessed
mpany him.

— Yusef Komunyakaa

All Peepal Tree titles are available from the website
www.peepaltreepress.com
with a money back guarantee, secure credit card ordering
and fast delivery throughout the world at cost or less.

Contact us at:
Peepal Tree Press, 17 King's Avenue, Leeds LS6 1QS, UK
Tel: +44 (0) 113 2451703 E-mail: contact@peepaltreepress.com

Chris Abani
Feed Me the Sun
ISBN: 9781845231569; pp. 196; pub. June 2010; £10.99

"In this eclectic and imaginative poetry book Chris Abani takes us on a time-travelling journey around the world. He explores history, war, myth, religion, relationships and a poet's personal and philosophical musings. His versatile voice is, variously, audacious, energetic, visual, oblique and always, always, thought-provoking."

Bernardine Evaristo

This collection of Chris Abani's longer poems, some previously published, many new, displays his astonishing energy, beauty of expression and range of reference to contemporary life, history, art and literature. Having this work together in one volume enables us to see the dialogue between a sense of the personal and an engagement with the public and historical, from 'Daphne's Lot' which explores the life of an Englishwoman (his mother) caught up in the madness of the Biafran civil war, or 'Buffalo Women', an epistolary sequence of poems between lovers caught up in the American civil war. The focus of Abani's poems is frequently on extreme situations where the unspeakable becomes too readily the doable, but where against the odds compassion and love remain and the individual determination to resist public madness. In 'Sanctificum' there is a profound meditation on the sacred, whether reached through religious ritual or through art, and the narrow dividing line between the urge to reach for mastery and transcendence and the abuses of power whether personal, contemporary or historical.

Marion Bethel
Bougainvillea Ringplay
ISBN: 9781845230845; pp. 88, July 2009; £7.99

These poems are sensual in the most literal sense – the poems are about the senses, the smell of vanilla and sex, the sound of waves – radio, voices, sea; the taste of crab soup; the texture of hurricane wind, and the chaos of colours bombarding the eye. Bahamian poetry is being defined in the work of Marion Bethel.

Jacqueline Bishop
Snapshots from Istanbul
ISBN: 9781845231149; pp. 80, April 2009; £7.99

Framed by poems that explore the lives of the exiled Roman poet Ovid, and the journeying painter Gaugin, Bishop, already between Jamaica and the USA, locates her own explorations of where home might be. This is tested in a sequence of sensuous poems about a doomed relationship in Istanbul, touching in its honesty and, though vivid in its portrayal of otherness, highly aware that the poems' true subject is the uprooted self.

Christian Campbell
Running the Dusk
ISBN: 9781845231552; pp. 84, June 2010; £8.99

Christian Campbell takes us to dusk, what the French call *l'heure entre chien et loup*, the hour between dog and wolf, to explore ambiguity and intersection, danger and desire, loss and possibility. These poems of wild imagination shift shape and shift generation, remapping Caribbean, British and African American geographies: Oxford becomes Oxfraud; Shabba Ranks duets with Césaire; Sidney Poitier is reconsidered in an exam question; market women hawk poetry beside knock-off Gucci bags; elegies for ancestors are also for land and sea. Here is dancing at the crossroads between reverence and irreverence. Dusk is memory, dusk is dream, dusk is a way to re-imagine the past.

Kwame Daw
Back of M
ISBN

Ishion Hutchinson
Far District
ISBN: 9781845231576; pp.

Far District explores a journey
the rural village, which the
and the world of western
the writer has felt shut
poverty. As the poet's j
the world of books an
"home" might offer
memory and the lite

Far District is a mar
does this collect
reaching image
psychological t
leap-frogging
engage the re
contagious
tion throu
lenged T
to jour
to acc

P
exp
discove
history,
reminder of

Above all,
begins in a prima
Monty hopes, 'the h
all relationships must
corruptions of knowledg

Millicent A.A. Graham
The Damp in Things
ISBN: 9781845230838; pp. 56, May

In *The Damp in Things*, we are invited into th
Millicent Graham: she offers us a way to see h
porary and urban Jamaica through the slant eye
willing to see the absurdities and contradictions
society. These are poems about family, love, spiritual
above all desire, where the dampness of things is as much
humid sensuality of this woman's island as it is about her c
belief in fecundity, fertility and the unruliness of the imagina
deeply aware of the value of both homage and resistance. The resu
is a wonderfully executed balancing act that ultimately suggests a
newness of sensibility and imagination.